# NIGHT DRAWINGS

Winner of the 1994 Marianne Moore Poetry Prize

The Marianne Moore Poetry Prize was established in 1991 by Helicon Nine, Inc., and is awarded annually to a previously unpublished manuscript chosen by a distinguished poet through an open, nationwide competition.

The judge for 1994 was David Ignatow.

# NIGHT DRAWINGS

*Poems*

MARJORIE STELMACH

With a Foreword by David Ignatow

HELICON NINE EDITIONS
KANSAS CITY, MISSOURI

Copyright © 1995 by Marjorie Stelmach

All rights reserved under International and Pan American Copyright Conventions. Published by Helicon Nine Editions, a division of Midwest Center for the Literary Arts, Inc., P.O. Box 22412, Kansas City, MO 64113.
Requests to copy any part of this work should be addressed to the publisher.

Certain of these poems first appeared in the following magazines and anthologies: *Ascent*; *Billee Murray Denny Awards Anthology* (1988-1989 and 1992-1993); *The Cape Rock*; *Chelsea*; *Cumberland Review*; *Gardening the Skies*, 1st Missouri Writers Biennial Awards Publication (1989); *Malahat Review*; *River Styx*; *Southern Poetry Review*; and *Union Street Review*.

Book design: Tim Barnhart
Cover photograph: Alfred Böschl

Partial funding for this book was provided by the National Endowment for the Arts, a federal agency, the Missouri Arts Council and the Kansas Arts Commission, state agencies; and the N.W. Dible Foundation.

Library of Congress Cataloging-in-Publication Data

Stelmach, Marjorie.
   Night drawings : poems / Marjorie Stelmach. -- 1st ed.
     p.   cm.
   ISBN 1-884235-12-3 (alk. paper)
   I. Title.
PS3569.T3798N5 1995
811'.54--dc20                                                   95-17175
                                                                                 CIP

FIRST EDITION
This book is printed on recycled, acid-free paper.
Printed in the United States of America.

HELICON NINE EDITIONS

*for Dan*

# Contents

*Foreword*  9

*Grace Notes*

    Grace Notes  13
    In Those Day  14
    Fire  15
    The Fisherman's Gift on Father's Day  16
    After Her Death  17
    Here Be Dragons  18
    At Twelve  20
    Her Father's Nightmare  23
    A Simple Weather  24
    Night Ritual  26
    Imagine a Man  27
    Confirmation  29
    Imagining Angels  30
    Calling Back the Dead  33
    What to Expect  34

*Doorways*

    Doorways  37

*Night Drawings*

    Night Drawings  55
    Playing the Long Joke  58
    Road House in Flood Season  60
    Somewhere Over Ireland  61
    Her Work  63

Permanent Setting  64
Yesterday's Story  67
The Face of the Idiot Moon  69
If I Get It Wrong  71
Two-Part Meditation  73
Pentecost  76
Draft of an Answer  80
Intercession  81
After the Service  83
The One Art that Changes Nothing  84
Facing Pages  86

*About the Author*  88

# Foreword

Generally, first books of poetry concern themselves with domestic and private life, and that is to the good. It affirms the self in the here and now, as the first step to self-understanding and understanding of the self in relation to others. It is process towards an overall view of the life lived, as all of us so deeply desire. In the act of achieving this vision, poems emerge as metaphors of our growing belief. Remarkably, they are the creative act itself finding in itself meaning in creativity. Such a total achievement takes a lifetime of work. Rarely, if ever, is it to be seen emerging in a first book, but as in everything, there is an exception, and that is *Night Drawings*.

I have read *Night Drawings* with intense interest, a prayerful book. Ordinary, everyday speech is transformed as a medium of reverence towards experience, that in which one must find meaning. The daily life is the key to and burden of the book, and a highly original and perceptive start it is. For example, there is the concept of the Door, a unique metaphor for the ambiguity in which one finds oneself in search of meaning. The Door open is meant as open to all and any events in the hope that it will also invite clarity in one's life. That it does not, in effect, is also the prayerful stance one meets in this book. As if with hands clasped before it, *Night Drawings* moves from moment to moment in search of significance supposedly to be found.

*Night Drawings* is permeated with this tension, and yet prayerfulness itself is meaning in sustaining hope and faith.

For a first book, *Night Drawings* is a signal achievement. Much more will need to be explored and understood in subsequent books by this talented poet to achieve the totality of vision the poet seeks, but as the book stands, it is a breakthrough for the author and for us, the readers, to the important work yet to come.

DAVID IGNATOW
*Judge*

*Grace Notes*

# Grace Notes

If a sparrow dies in flight, the sky
turns inside out accepting it.
A feather may drift about for days
to mark a moving plot
with the thin blade of a name.
But no sparrow falls.

Dimly prescient, sparrows cup their seeds
in fragile domes hollow as heavens.
In time the skies crack
and grow wide with fledglings.
Winged like eighth notes,
they hold in hollowed bones
space enough for a grave
should grace prove too slow.

# In Those Days

I think of love itself as different in those earlier days
of dirt roads and window fans. I think of it
as slow. Love on a slow climb, like bees at work
in loops up long slopes of goldenrod, or ropes
of roses opening on trellises, or a hired man,
half-way up a ladder, leaning, gazing off toward town,
everything ascending. And a calm woman facing the sky
while her man climbs up from the fields, past a sun
sinking toward dinnertime. I think of love as the line
of his steady climb, never to cross the line of her eyes, and lust
as the urgency of lives lived at the pace of seasons—
his hat on the doorknob, her apron on a chair, and their hot skin
dried by the breeze that walks the second-story sky
to rest in the small of his back where her hand has been, to pause
at the base of her throat where his face was pressed. I think
love must have been different then, something for the light
to take with it when it left, as it takes the bright dust
of the air, the flowers on the spread, the corners of their mouths
as they come down for supper—he with his clean hands,
her hands behind her back, tying the apron sash.
I think of love as the still hour before supper, the spareness
of the cooling room, the slow risk of a need so well understood,
it has long been agreed upon, and they can take their fill
of food that has been growing all this time, unattended in fields
rising in gardens, ripening on sills, and sleep as if love
were no different from what it had always been, as if
they never had to think of love at all.

# Fire

Hot wine and the season's first fire.
We imagine how we might begin again, watching
light fray the dark back to the same love
we remember losing.

All night we sip the smoke of wine till thirst
dies and our eyes burn open.
It's solitude we love. Our bodies
shape hard dark, their edges
lit and smoking. Separate
as only light can make us, we dream
soft dreams of ashes.

# The Fisherman's Gift on Father's Day

Later there will be light meat, lemon, and a dry white wine,
but first this fish: one round eye, jaw stuck out refusing death.
Its wedged muscle thrusts against the vise of his hand
as if the air held currents of escape. His daughters wince
as he hefts his Father's Day knife by the blade, pauses
at the level of their eyes, and cracks the handle down
across its skull, hard, three times.

The fourth blow ends it.
He releases his pent breath and his grip on the blade,
reverses it in his hand, turns it to its purpose.
His daughters always ask the sex so he probes the luminous guts,
draws out the dark ovaries, splayed on the knife edge,
but they can't look.

Tooth-shaped scales lodge in porch cracks,
glistening under the light of hung lamps.
He watches them all evening as other men might stare
into fires or at stars. When the girls are asleep
he lifts his glass, turning the thin stem, watching the wine
cast scales of light on the dark rafters.

Pressing the arc of his rocker down over land that was water once,
he feels currents pass beneath the floorboards
and wonders what it is that builds
such stubbornness into a life, when every breath
is a gasp of lethal air. He wonders
what tool a man would need to break that hold,
something he doesn't own, something
he wouldn't know how to ask for.

# After Her Death

The lake is growing still. The father leans
back from his children, breaking the circle,
and lifts both arms above them. When he smiles
they know they will lose him to the lake.
As he wraps himself in a flannel jacket
and life vest, they feel the cold he goes to.

They stay indoors and listen to the rasp
of tackle box on wooden slats, the ring
of the dropped chain, the grainy shove
of an oar as he pushes off into mist,
watch until he blends with the black wedge
of the boat, and only the oars break
into light. When the last ripples
reach shore, they put themselves to bed.

Hours later he docks and drapes the chain
around the mooring, folding each loop over the last
so as not to wake them. When he climbs
into the loft, the lake rises with him. Even in sleep,
their eyelids lift to his presence, revealing
black pools where his moving shadow disturbs
the spreading circles of a larger absence.

# Here Be Dragons

I.
My brother writes that he's moving again,
down from the mountains
where he took up healing,
wrote essays on solitude,
raised goats.

He's heading north to a state that hangs out
like a flat orange tongue,
a state fit only for hamstrung cattle,
community newsletters,
fat-bodied flies.

His letters worry my dreams and I wake
panicked about—his goats?
How does he choose what to leave?

Up past midnight I study old texts:
folk medicine, home healing
(peppermint for depression, clove
for lost love) hoping to stumble
on our family sickness.

It isn't distance.
This world's not so large I can't handle it
in dreams. Awake, I want things to stay put.
I've marked the map above my desk—an X
for each of us. Rivers drip on my blotter.

As for me, I hug myself so tight,
a crease cuts my heart like a fault line.

II.
Across the room my map hangs reversed
in the dark glass,
sky lapping at the edges where seas should be,
and my face rising, a dragon in the heartland,
wearing the family features.
In the black of my eyes, stars swim in circles.
Along the coastlines, cities turn
to runes; in the outlands, borders rise and run off
into the sky,
where no one is sure-footed.

And so I stay at home and gather signs
like everybody else—
bits of the universe believed
to heal the heart as saffron heals the blood.

It isn't easy keeping the heart whole, in a world
where every piece of earth is named already,
and every X on the map is someone's name
for solitude. Tonight
I have names for each of us, and in my face
the family features hold,
strong enough to guard the heartland. But at dawn
the sky will rise like subterranean waters
to erase the map and fill my eyes
with light. There is no cure.

*Write soon. Take care.*
Here be dragons. Here.

# At Twelve

> At Twelve: Portraits of Young Women, Sally Mann

She is not dressed for going.
Barefoot in cotton nightdress and open
robe, one arm at rest behind her on the thin wire rail,
hand closed on the opposite cable,
she leans, she sways,
halfway across the crude board bridge.
If something is about to happen,
here is one of the sad places
it will choose to begin.

The language of the photograph is simple:
a shape we read as *flesh* (as us),
stands on a bridge.
Below her, a *force*—a rush of current,
arrested, turned to pumice—a visual code
for flow and stone resistance.
In the world's language, it's a short step
from this to sex:
light, cast like a first stone.

Or myth: from the upper right, a steep slant of sun
forms a second bridge, oblique
and thick enough to have borne
the heavy-bodied immortals down
into once-bearable lives.
At the base, a woman, cradled by wire mesh
and washed by a shower that would be gold,
if gods still lusted for the direct
gaze of the barely-born-human soul.

Even in this godless day,
it's a lit and stern soul that slouches,
wholly adolescent, above a full-grown river—

fierce and fast—perhaps the Shenandoah itself.
In the clearing behind her (always a clearing,
like the world's peremptory throat),
stands the plain white house she came from—
brick chimney, square windows, centered door.
It is not where she's going.

Though she's not dressed for going,
going seems to be the point.
Page after page of children, born
between the Blue Ridge and Allegheny ranges,
brought by the cut of the shutter to the brink
of going. Twelve years old. The eyes
carry histories, how each one rose, a mix
of dark and disaster (dark and desire)
from which the invisible slipped

like a cloak.
From this, it's a short step
to flesh and blood—and blood
and light—and blood again:
a woman's life. The language
of photography is simple: we know
this is not *now*, but only one of the sad
places *now* goes.
We have all dressed for going,

all of us wearing the under-hum,
the heart's stumble and hold, the skin's
quickened surface—that lift of flesh and gold
to the brush of the Significant.
Before our eyes, she bares the beginning
of a woman's face. In the space before her,
a second woman tightens a lens. The force
of a single finger comes down and flesh
lights here, on this page.

Now she meets *our* gaze, wearing the face
she'll wear when she joins us here,
this side of the photo's border—

a few years older, a little less
accessible to light, knowing the instant
of the shutter's drop for what it was: a rape,
that furious vision of oneself as chosen—and so,
repeatable (the rape, the vision)
each time she looks.

And she'll never stop looking.
When time has altered her face
into a force,
has worked its way into the shadows
of her lips and wrists, and she has grown
more aware of angles, the dangerous fall
of light through the thin
cloth of nightclothes—still,
she'll look. Because

it has always been about sex: a willingness
to stand in that sticky spotlight
we read every time as god's spilled gold;
to be taken like a photo, once and for all,
with light the only document and no proof
but us—the thousands of us even now turning
the page. We don't even wish
to stop it. It is, after all, the approach
of the Significant; the Something

about to happen.
We watch and let the myths shiver
in the backstage dark. We turn
the page. (We have turned the page:
a black bridge falling through an arc of darkening
air; a young woman's face pressed to a sheet
of quenched light, a sound
like a single wing.) Another child
on the next page.

# Her Father's Nightmare

When she wakes straight up screaming, he is there,
his weight on her bed, his gravity against her.
Father and daughter, eyes narrowed to the glare
of midnight. Something huge, she says.
He has no answer.

He watches his face stretch across her eyes
while in the world behind, something huge draws back
and yes it was just a dream and yes she's fine
and yes yes he can go.

No she is not fine. He knows
this time she won't call—knows
he's lost her.
From his dreams he'll watch her
sink toward her own center—no one's daughter
while the beast gathers in all the corners.

# A Simple Weather

Rain runs the streets of the steep river town,
falls into itself in the warehouse lot
where motors start hot and throaty,
loosens the oldest gravestones, and
softens the sills of the upstairs room
where all afternoon the two have made love
watching for the rain to stop or to continue,
watching each other for something like weather.
Now streetlights come on, angling silver
into the room where he has left her.
She has agreed to take what comes. What more
could the world have offered beyond
the simple weather of this room, after.

Night edges downstream; he drives upstate
toward home. She pictures him peering
through rain-slashed glass
where wipers drag arcs across his face
leaving neon bruises. A paste
of elongated letters smears
the slick road behind him. She knows
she has let this go
too far. But her palms smell of him,
and rain still falls across her sills.
It touches her face and throat as she kneels,
watching for the pain to stop
or to continue.

Out on the river,
sandbars take what comes, as always.
Rain will fall all night upon them,
as the river falls south into the Gulf
that falls, itself, off ocean edges
toward depths with no weather she can imagine.
Instead, she imagines herself a sandbar

taking the rain into her skin
because it has come tonight to the river,
has come to her with enough force
to carry off bits of what she believes
to be herself. Again tonight
she'll dream herself smaller and wake believing
it doesn't matter—what stays, what goes.
She knows this is all the world can offer;
still she imagines that far, far downstream
the weather is simpler.

# Night Ritual

Finger things: a silver hook
lifted and lowered on the screen-porch door,
a lamp-key turned to lower the flame,
a gown's hem lifted for stairs, one
slippered foot suspended.
                        And soon,
in a room at the top of the stairs
a curtain drawn back, eyes raised to find
the absence or shape
of the moon's silver hook.
                        Always
the same position—there,
in the lattice of limbs,
always the same time: alone.

# Imagine a Man

with time on his hands
and the key to a room
where a woman's tears
can fall like night
having nothing at all
to do with him.

Imagine his hands
filling with tears;
he lifts them, turns them
watching light break
into fragile globes
as he lets her tears
slip along veins
over wrists down arms
toward his waiting
heart.

Imagine his window
filling with wings
as birds flock back
to snow-packed fields
because it's time
and the sky turns black
with a thousand hearts
and no air between them.

Imagine a sun
that cracks like an egg
till red light drips
off wings down walls
over windows where women
fill dry eyes
and behind them,

men wait
with cupped hearts.

Imagine a city
awash with birds
red with a light
that burns itself off
the edge of a world
it never loved
even now
as the woman turns
to a man she imagines
is waiting to touch her
with time, only time,
on his hands.

# Confirmation

Each time it comes into the world, rain
reinvents air out of nothing
with the kindest hands imaginable,
the finest inclinations.
Slowly, out of the silence come
catalpas, wet and heavy-lidded,
brushing the eaves of the sleeping porch.
And slowly out of the dark come balsams
shifting syllables like slow prayers.
Then, out of nothing at all, come lines
softly curving across the planes
of our sleepy faces, waves
of water-light washed from dreams
where men are long-hearted and recall
the look of the world before all
this accuracy.

# Imagining Angels

> *"Be ahead of all partings."*
> —Rainer Maria Rilke

I.
Rilke, the angels are stiff with years;
they barely move.
Wings worn down to wedges,
when they sleep in snow, they leave,
no sweeping arcs like before, but dents,
not unlike hoofprints.

When I find their traces now
I remember a quaint frontispiece:
a forest clearing, a spill of light,
a small child bearing
a block of salt, and hidden in the trees,
the gentle guest, come at last,

ears flicking a touchingly transparent
gratitude in return for—what?
Was it only silence the angels asked?
A willingness to watch? Our absence
from the clearing?
Not very much, after all. And now,

deer, too, are hard to come by,
rare as gentleness itself;
and so much else, lost:
the forest, an empty cathedral, left
to its own light; the saltlick,
one more sorcery outgrown.

Tell me, Rilke,
what shape love leaves these days
in snow. I've been calling and calling.

But the fields stretch so unbroken
I can only conclude the angels are older,
the angels are dying.

II.
A man I have always loved
loves God, has loved this one thing
for a century. I imagine him,
walking the small distance down the lawn
for mail—a summoning
of strength, a cane.

I see him on tiptoe, leaving
no mark in the grass,
his slight weight pressed
on the cane's rubber tip: perfect circles.
Angel prints. Daily,
this brief foray of grace, and then,

the return—longer, more perilous,
his bones thinned
from a hundred years of small tasks:
leading evening prayers,
clearing snow from the church walk, kneeling
beside children reading tracks.

Imagining this, I find myself whispering:
*Angels Angels.*
A man I have always loved is preparing now.
His weight floats in my arms; he leans
toward the light, listening
for the oldest answer: wings approaching.

In the face of this call,
human love must seem no more
than a clearing, where some last kindness
may still enter.
A man I love is leaving now, taking
his one love with him.

When he's gone, I fear the angels
will not be called back. Left
to our own devices under the icy stars,
we'll lose that part of our story, the frontispiece
reminding us of a love that could once be drawn
by the salt of our tracks.

We'll move through the forest talking aloud,
explaining as best we can
that there are simply too many of us,
we never asked
to be visited by a gentleness
that would leave these prints in our hearts.

Rilke, the angels have left us
for spaces where we know nothing
exists. Rilke, *the angels, the angels*
have left us. Without them,
the weight of our bodies will kill us.
The weightlessness of our souls.

# Calling Back the Dead

And why? It's not as if we are kind —
speaking always ill. It's not as if
we're above morbid fascination
or worse, rude lapses
of attention.

Besides: they'd see us at our worst.
Scavenging our mirrors, picking at
the privacies of dream, ungainly
in our beds, worrying ourselves to death
like beads.

Consider the difference: we lump, while they
wear auras like shivering troutskin, speak
wind bells, touch luminescent, make meaning
like love, smell no longer of diseases
they will die of.

Ask yourself why. Kneel
and ask it. Ask quietly, *Why?*
Listen hard. Then say it—
the answer. Say it:
*Goodbye.*

# What to Expect

We know what we have the right to expect:
long waits on welcome mats, blank looks
from bank and fortune tellers.

We've seen how it is with the world:
long faces in church, long gaps
between letters, and longing. Longing.

But love. We expect love.
It doesn't seem reasonable not to
these days when so little suffices. And so

we move through tiers of strangers, alert
for the lifted lashes of those
we somehow expect to be kissed by. Ah yes —

we have expectations. But then, we expect them
to fail, for so the sad histories tell us.
And more and more it seems doubtful

that wishes are horses. Beggars we're born
and we'll die with our cups in our hands.
It's right that we die. We expect it.

But gods. We expect gods.

*Doorways*

# Doorways

## I. In other people's dreams

I appear in doorways. I always know
something they should know.
I call them in to hear the tidings, or out
to watch the world do whatever it's doing.
Sometimes I've come to warn them—*No.
Don't look: the shuttle's crashed;
the beautiful child's stillborn; wait,
the stairway's gone.*
Then I vanish or my words wake them.
Either way, my part is over.

It's a gift of sorts, a calling: I appear
and disappear my body like a wink
or a moon,
thin into rooms and out,
as if my cells could take the shapes
of ornamental spaces in the lacework of worlds.

Meanwhile, in my own dreams I move slow motion.
Dreamfields unfold like lifetimes before me;
buffeted by landscapes, I can't seem to fly.
I watch my doorways fill
with clear gaps where no one stands,
and never will again. I listen.
No word comes.

After years of being told at breakfast or in letters
of my appearances,
I've begun to feel an awkwardness in living.
Our comings and goings, the expansions
and contractions of the air between us,
these cumbersome tissues we call our lives,
how could these be real?

And dreams?
Words spoken in dreams stay
or they don't. Screams
doppler off into breakfasts,
words of comfort sink into the sweetened milk.
If, in broad day we suddenly turn
and look over our shoulders at doorways,
it's nothing. We know we're alone;
but sometimes
we think we may not be.

## II. I've set myself the Doorway Task:

*As you pass through a doorway, remember yourself.*

I miss three a day on my way to breakfast. No concentration.
But if I keep at it, I tell myself, and garner each doorway,
I will have collected no less than my life.

*I keep at it; I learn I'm no good at this.*

Men are collectors; they go all out:
comic books, train models, postage stamps, guns,
cigar-store Indians, World War I planes.

*What I collect: ones.*

One pewter napkin ring. One old city map. One translucent vase
from one world's fair. One kaleidoscope. One friend. One mask.
No true collector, I accumulate.

*Accumulator: Dark body in deep space, storing up power? Yes.*

And the Doorway Task? The work continues.
One day I'll come to myself in one doorway.
"Me," I'll say. "Whole. In this doorway. This moment."

*And know what I'm doing this for, and be done with it.*

## III. Cells

i. She stands at the far end of the dock.

When I come, we move off onto the lake. Afraid
I'll capsize us both, I ask questions,
polite and trembling: *like this? is this right?*
*When will I ever be good at this, ever*
*learn balance?*

Never speaking above a whisper, perhaps
not even aloud,
I grip the belt of her jeans.
Her white shirt—my father's shirt—
billows and softens my face.
She answers: *Don't worry.*
*Nothing you do could be wrong.*

ii. Sometimes I hear my mother's life whisper

from the edge of my cells: *die now.*
And I see her that day—her doctor,
white in the doorway with truth
in an envelope, wordless.
She and her doctor
are crying. Both women,
crying. When, soon,
they stop crying, one of them knows
when her life will be over. The other
has told her.

Not crying, my father quietly closes
the doors between us the morning he tells us
the truth, and I run
to press my face to her pillow.
As I fall, the white cotton billows. I know
there will be no talk of this. Ever.
A smooth lake, rising. Lives have fallen

beneath this surface.
I know one is his. I think
one is mine.

iii.  These days no one dies

of that message. Doctors
stride across thresholds
with programs of treatment.
A blessing. But still, I stand here awake
in the doorway between our two lives,
calling after her.

Reaching the age of her death now,
forever her daughter, her elder—my hands
equally empty of pain and of healing,
no daughter to whisper to
*nothing you do could be wrong*—
I watch the doorways where truth is expected
and know I'll never be good at this—ever.

## IV. Revolving Doors

Book 1: A history

of hermetic sins: a man
at the door of Diana's place, clearing
his throat like a clod. *Lay down
the bow*, he thinks—
*and quickly*. Not quickly
enough.           Art at Susannah's.
The old men gather
to gape at flesh. Dirt
clogs their shuffle. Breeding
requires they lower their eyes
to the dust. Instead, and shortly,
they'll lower themselves.
                    Sailors
come clomping to muck up the garden,
one foot off the craft and cursing
their luck, sweating like cool white gold
in a tropical forest. The New World—
but *get the hell out*
is all they want. Already
too late.

Turned on and torn to shreds
by their own, returning—hounds,
history, hormones—
they looked on Beauty, and Death
damned their eyes.
This isn't the Word I stand here bearing.
This is Witness: our undoing.

Book 2: A tale

of Bluebeard as Godhead,
in which we find
a doorway lined with dark and a key
slipped under the welcome mat.
That story. Yes.
So, riddle me this:
How can a beaver rebuild
when the whole damn river
is over? How can a sky reopen after
it's bombed at the box office? How
can a born-again world turn over
a new leaf after the fall?
No answer?

Then give me your first born,
I'll name her Gaia, she'll grow up lovely
on pointlessness.
Pricking her finger at last, she'll sleep
the sleep of the just
married—and we'll all sleep with her
till somebody comes
who can love her, can cut
through the riddles, can get
to the thorns.

\*

Or better, a Fish Tale. Old bass,
eyeless or hook-marred
or otherwise scarred by the coming
of men and the sons
of men—these
are closed doors.
And this is the Law:
let them pass back into the waters,
lower, release them, leave them
for others.

And if you're a quiet believer, leave
your hand in the water and feel them
moving their whole world into your palm.
In return, three wishes: two waves
from the spine's sweet two-sided curve
washing over your fingers and wrist; and third,
the palm's weightlessness
as you return your flesh
to the air. Come true.

\*

Or the Wonderland story, where once a doorway
opened wide in a garden wall and we
were OUT—Alice, too, wanted back
and shrunk down into that small
view of herself with which we're familiar.
Soon, the only way back
was to click our heels three times and imagine
no place like home. But three clicks
is never far enough from the clearing. In fact,
no clearing appears in the forecast.
It's all the same
weather, now, in this world.

## V. Rooms roped off

Emily's room, the Alcotts' parlor,
Tom Edison's lab, Tom Sawyer's cave.
Summer. Everywhere guides stand in doorways
repeating themselves across the world.
We trail them through the homes of the famous,
viewing the treasures: the baby's
sweet hand-carved cradle, the quaint
chamber pots, the washstands
and quill pens.
                Willingly, we go through contortions:
climb spiral stairs to observatories; stoop to enter
fall-out shelters; clamber down ladders
to gape at the quarters of galley slaves; cringe
at foul-looking metal in Civil War hospitals,
vials in turn-of-the-century labs.

But we always return to the bedrooms,
quieted there by the quilted spreads,
shawls folded over the ladderback chairs,
needlepoint backings on oval brushes,
the soft grain of tortoiseshell combs.
Generations of privacies: women and men
crossing thresholds at evening, pausing
to sigh: a day well spent or well over.
We can imagine.
                As sometimes, too,
we imagine a future of ghosts at our doorways
imagining us. A fair telling
of the human story: men and women
repeating themselves down the ages, pausing
at roped-off doorways to think themselves
into other lives, while daily they pass
through their own doorways, thinking
of nothing.

## VI. The lost rooms list

Conservatory, library, parlor, study.
Drawing room, garret, milady's chambers.
Wine cellar, pantry, butler's apartment,
servants' quarters, banquet halls, chamberlain's suite.
Billiard rooms, ballrooms.
Expansiveness and craft.
All of them lost. All of it over.

And vanished institutions:
poorhouses, work farms, old folks homes,
asylums, madhouses, all but gone,
their names changed, their new locations
largely unknown. What remain
are the doorways the nameless ones find—
must find—on their own.

And last, the gas and torture chambers
abandoned now for prison cells
with bare interrogation rooms
below—and more
(so vast, our needs)
huge rooms without doors, variously called:
exile, abandonment, the killing fields.

# VII. Definitions, efficient and inefficient

### i. The uses of doorways

From a window
you can leap to your death, look down
on a crowd, catch lovers on a rooftop
in the act, start the 30 Years' War. From a door,
you can't.

In a doorway, you become a *presence*.
Paused as an equinox:
*composed; between*. Nothing
can happen. Lean
either way and the moment's gone.


### ii. Doorways as attitudes of denial

*Here, but not me.*

I have come in disguise,
a demon, an angel,
a god to test your welcome;
to bless you;
to kill you.

*Me, but not here.*

Yes, you are honored.
It goes without saying; announce me
with rose petals, trumpets,
stunned silence.
Don't think I'm staying.

*Me, here, but not now.*

Gate crasher, bad fairy,
down-and-out kin,

boorish neighbor, bill collector.
*Not a good time?* I'm off then, but first
there's some business.


iii. Doorways as lovers

No reason. We love them.
They rhyme of their own
doing, like mirrors.
After a time, they seem to fit us, even
become us. Two-way dreams:
nothing without us.

## VIII. The danger in doorways

They line our dreams—metaphors
for our metaphors,
the thresholds of choice,

of change: the door of the eclipse
through which the sun passes,
like a Klein bottle, into itself;

the door of the solstice
where time is tricked
into seasons that don't exist

and will kill us;
and more than a thousand light years away,
a door that's Bluebearded up

full of long-dead light
that nonetheless twinkles.
Some doorways are sealed.

Not many. By doorways,
leaves enter the air,
rain fills the raindrop,

ears open to echoes, eyes
to the light, skin to touch.
Flesh opens to love

and we open the future.
You, my doorway, open me,
with hands I've dreamt a million times,

your flesh, a door that opens on falling
through endless doorways
inside me.

And borne through the safest
of doorways, a daughter—and on:
the daughters of daughters of daughters.

Which of our many names
will sound the farthest sound they hear
as they sift back the years

through deflected light,
seeking the one small door in the garden,
through which they entered

the mind of the world?
And sons,
and the sons of our sons,

millions of seeds breaking back
through the sound
of unaltered syllables.

Will they know more of doorways,
or less, being men? By then,
will names be doors

for our daughters,
as now they are drawn
bolts?

The only answer is the one I open
myself, in you,
to love and through death.

At last to walk
through the needle obelisk,
no eye enough to hold us,

silver spinning us to silver
until we are fine
and can pass, aching

between the ache
and the lack
into . . .

The danger in doorways:
they imply a room
beyond.

## IX. In other people's dreams, they tell me

doorways open into sky—
a thousand dreamers rising

over unfamiliar landscapes
they know to be their own.

Do they feel a lightening of flesh?
muscle-pull at take-off? a tightening of sinew?

Do they breathe, aloft, more fully
or fall breathless in the lift

and bewilderment of currents?
Do their wings open simply—like eyes,

one more way of seeing, easing
the world into distance and back

into drama? How does it feel
to fly? to come to yourself

in that doorway?
buffeted by love, to rise?

Balanced here on the edge of earth,
awake, looking up, I ask it again,

as wind and sun come falling
through doorways. Some days,

I look over my shoulder: I think we're alone;
we may not be.

*Night Drawings*

# Night Drawings

begin as notes—a phone number or a time,
a street address on a Mondrian map.
But when she returns to the tablet, late,
the message waits, disembodied like
his lullaby voice saying love, long-distance,
in all his ways.
                    She picks up the pencil
and, eyes half-closed, darkens the 7
to a wedge—black, slick—moves on
to the 4, turning meaning to pure
cuneiform—soon, the 1
is the darkest street in the city.
His voice moves over her, and *yes*
she whispers, *I know*—wondering
what he has said, lifting her pencil, lowering it
to a clean part of the sheet.
                            Eyes,
she draws, always.
They lengthen, deepen under her hand,
returned from another world having seen
dark prints on the underside of the sea,
the turn of the moon down over its own
disk, palm-flesh pressed to the bones
of a face. Now tears fall tear-shaped in links
toward the shaled edge of the tablet.
                                And
*What are you thinking?* he is asking.
She's thinking trees. She tells him *Nothing,
love, nothing.* The trunk lines carry
a heavy shadow. She moves her pencil
over and over down long left edges,
layering bark with the side of the lead.
Roots twist over the eyes, become
gruff brows and furrows; the eyes age,

entangled there in the roots—ancient eyes
looking up from soil.
                        Shaken, she laughs,
and his sentence breaks. *What is it ?*
he asks. *Nothing, my love,* she says,
*I was just thinking.* The edge
of her hand is smudged. It has pressed
a charcoal crescent over her cheek bone.
But she can't see this, and soon her face
is all one color, her window black;
her wineglass holds the last cone
of moon.
            His voice comes back.
*Shall I hang up, then, let you sleep?*
*Are you still lonely or can you sleep?*
*Yes*, she says, watching grey light sink
further into the softening paper.
She is drawing branches. They spread
and drop leaves on the dark city map,
a fetid blanket, smelling at once of death
and spring. As she draws tiny seedcups,
the whole sheet silvers in risen moon.
He whispers her name, a question.
                                It falls
into the streets where leaves lift to it,
gathers in furrows between the eyes,
sinks into eyebrows, settles. Tree roots
drink tearshapes. Soon she will sleep
in the city of his voice. But first
she presses the flattened lead hard,
moves her hand in an arc.
A circle. Then slower,
riding a curve cut by branches.
It deepens, cuts branches,
cuts deeper, and down
into layers of paper.
                    By the time
she has cut the first sheets

the receiver rests on her pillow.
She hears his voice as the days pass
on the sheet and the moon she is drawing
goes dark. Everywhere, eyes
are closed at the roots.
                         He says,
*sleep well, my love.* But she
keeps circling down through layers, until
the circle is deeper than paper.
She sees how the world has left
its number. Her palm
falls open, and she hears nothing
when finally he cradles the phone.
In her dream: a mouth, a cypher, a moon.
In her dream, all leaves are numbered.

# Playing the Long Joke

> "There is a rite of imitation in which a band of people from one tribe, Arikara, for example, would imitate a band from some other tribe for long periods of time, fifteen years or more. They began doing this on the Northern plains in the 1820's, imitating each other in exacting detail, as a form of amusement. . . . playing the Long Joke."
> —Barry Holstun Lopez

One morning it begins, all of us at once becoming you.
We cast off our accustomed robes and dress in your manner,
wrap our skins tighter on our shoulders, make small tucks
in our sleeves. We confine ourselves to dove and russet tones,
shunning the lovely cerulean dyes brought from the hills
where we send our sons to hear the laughter of the gods
and come home men.
One morning we wake restless; it begins.

Our elders teach us what they know of your ways.
As our children sleep, we whisper your histories into their ears.
We shake seed rattles above their faces, sifting your rhythms
into their dreams, until your heroes rise from the dust
to instruct them in the art of dance. It's not enough.
We train our furtive sons to steal into your camps and send back word.
We sacrifice our daughters to your marriage beds in trade
for your privacies, the postures of your solitude.

In the early years we help each other adjust a pleat,
correct the angle of an elbow, add salt. But soon
we have only to watch each other, and only rarely do we glimpse
our former selves disappearing into the eyes of the elders.
When we begin to smell like you, our spies come home
where we submit them to subtle tortures of your design,
admonishing our young to master
the dismissive smile with which you honor death.

In the final years we breed your priests—
misfits, fools in loose blue robes,

who visit the forbidden hills and come home mad. Soon
we'll bear your savior, one who'll laugh and slap his thighs
and call us home
where you live now, or have always lived,
lying in wait.
Some of us will go.

# Road House in Flood Season

The only road left circles once around the place
and leaves the way it came.
Below, down a steep grade of long grass and weed trees,
the river drags past in one of its ugly moods.
Two artists rent the second floor—two studios,
one bed in an alcove off the hall,
and no one in the rooms below but cats
and the ghosts of whores.

All winter he works and reworks her portrait,
getting it wrong, scraping it off
until the canvas sags with a worked-in residue
and there's no getting it right.
All winter she sits for him,
watching the river in shallowing light.
Long before he sees it coming, she knows
he'll marry her, but not here and not yet.

All night while he waits in the narrow bed,
she paints what she sees: catfish
steering in luminous skin downstream,
past cats alert on the banks, their teeth
turned to palette knives, their eyes to tubes
of saffron, cadmium, cinder, bone.
Upriver, spring floods lug wreckage down
to where she waits, painting one shape:

a simple fish, a cat's eye,
half of infinity emptying out
into saffron, cadmium, cinder, bone.
Long before he sees it coming, she knows
the smooth curve the river will take
when it moves downcountry,
that bone is spring's color, that her face
is nearly done.

# Somewhere Over Ireland

I confess, I'm afraid about airports,
how terrorists leave unattended
the bags with the plastic explosives—and more,
how polite they can be mid-air,
sharing the arm rest,
smiling on smoothly rotating collars,
their cuffs shot with light to make me think: *silk*.
And then, there's the possible loss of engines.
When I close my eyes, I hear the howls
of the terrified, all of us sounding the same,
with the same last name, in the first light,
somewhere over Ireland. Toward dawn
I shiver, hug the thin comforter
tight to my shoulders. As always, I'm not prepared:
no labeled linens, no monogrammed luggage,
nothing but love to fall back on,
a short list of names, the slim chance
that someone below might distinguish
my howl from the rest as I pass
through a disappointment of clouds,
of travelers' cheques floating down,
the thin plastic cups, the oxygen masks
the film from the in-flight movie—specks
in a cold lack of color that could be the sky
over Ireland.
                  And why? Is it only because of
the teacups, shaped for the ladylike lift
that's all wrist and thin fingerbone?
Did all this begin when I caught myself
taking small sips and thinking *bone china*?
Or is it because the few words left
from my high school French
have begun to visit my dreams, dressed up
like Gertrude Stein in capacious black:

*S'il vous plaît*, and *merci*, they murmur.
*Ce n'est pas le temps. Impossible.*
A dark vocabulary, knit
on needles of rain under drawingroom light.
*Mais, non. Il n'y a pas de temps.*
I'm too old to travel, unraveling
here alone in the sky,
fiercely knitting on shrinking bones,
the shiver I'll wear to my death, if it comes.
And it will.
                And, Yes.
I'll meet you in Paris.
It won't be impossible. It will be
April. Above us
the buds will decide how to take it.
They do this each year.
My bones are less certain.
Perhaps, they'll fill and swell with spring,
and we'll find a way to blossom each other.
High over Ireland, I feel them try, even now,
to be wings.
It's not the hardness of Earth I fear,
though it's hard enough.
It's the falling away. When I breathe
the damp stars swell on the glass, and the best I can ask
is the cold clutch of terror returning, that old
comforter I've loved all along
on my bed of strange silks, on my bed
of drawn swords carefully placed each night
between me
and my terrorist lifetime, who smiles even now
(the width of an arm rest away) somewhere
above Ireland, ticking
like any heart that's been left
unattended.

# Her Work

In the charcoals, no one plows the fields.
No warriors pace the barricades. No children
race their hoops down streets toward a clean point
of convergence. At most, a silhouette appears
in the lit doorway of a settlement.
Out on a twilight river a tiny boy-shape bends
at the oars of a wooden boat.
Or a solitary man stands lost in thought
on the far side of a lake so rife with light
it calls his existence into question.

Oils, too: drape-darkened bedrooms, stiff
with mitered corners; libraries washed by moonlight,
shelves of blood-red spines and pages golden
at the cut; a kitchen caught midmorning,
leaf-shadows on the tiles, a table set
with napkin rings that cast ellipses onto folded linen;
a front guest closet, opened on a wedge of winter,
a bare lightbulb, a bar of wire shoulders,
frigid air rising from ankle holes of boots.
\*
Along the Northern coast of a landlocked sea,
the artist parks outside a small café
to wait for the dawn ferry—a vague
woman-shape on a windshield, sketching.
The regulars have gathered at her back,
their light behind her now, oblique.
How patiently they sit for her, sipping coffee,
gazing out past an **OPEN** sign turned earlier
—the whole world **CLOSED**. She knows
the shape of them, their seams and flaws,
is almost finished here. She presses
a soft lead seam onto a softening page;
a ferry rises shoreward
out of the flaws in the horizontal.

# Permanent Setting

i.
On this post card, one
bird in a hedgerow will think two
notes, an interval exactly equaling the space
between the sun and
sunset. On one of the three

benches that border the cinder paths,
a woman will sit bowed, a forearm
resting along one thigh, her fingers
weaving her straight-cut hair.
We cannot see

her face exactly. She will seem to be
watching the long clean cut
of the green horizon; her eyes will drop
over the edge—there, precisely
where the world stops

and the air opens. She will seem
to be calm. Directly above her,
a small disk of sun
will stare at something
straight ahead

in all directions; all directions
will seem dangerous.
Neat cinder paths will lead
precisely there
and the woman will not take them

will not even think
of taking them. Nothing will cross
her mind, no time will pass
in this still world that wears
a vaguely foreign face,

no time will move
the hand through her hair, no blink
obliterate the horizon. The light
is a fact beyond
all reason.

She will not breathe,
even when she feels
a sixth sense open
like a hand,
even when she sees—

somewhere inside her?
somewhere outside her?—
a crease cut the flesh
of a huge,
dimensionless sun.

It will swallow her.
Seven years will pass
on the card's blank side,
where words are meant
to appear.

ii.
No time
will have passed in the straight-cut dark,
when a three-dimensional woman opens
the drawer, to find the post card:
forgotten garden, calm-looking woman.

Brought back to light,
the woman will sit in her garden,
still bowed and faceless,
beside a stilled bird, while the flesh
of a second sun floats —

as before? as always?
No cell of skin is the same
in the hand
of the three-dimensional woman
who lifted this scene from a rack

seven years ago now,
and thought Yes,
for some reason forgotten,
and paid the small price
forever. Perhaps

she had something to say
at the time, or the painted woman,
calm in her garden,
seemed proof then
of something no longer

worth proving. Perhaps
any number of things.
But now
in that garden so timeless
it reads like the blank

side of a postcard,
the faceless woman has lost
the calm, has seen
something huge and moving
—above? within?—

a second coming
of flesh-colored light
like fingers of sun that entered
and filled
the four stilled chambers

of her straight-cut heart.
And now,
on the third side of the card,
a heartbeat begins—two notes:
and no time

between them,
a single eternal interval,
passing
between the sun
and its permanent setting.

# Yesterday's Story

The story today is about a stone
so carefully polished you'd swear
the sea had a hand in it,
if you didn't know the cutter
and hadn't fallen straight in love
with his handsome, blue-eyed boy,

who turned his own hand early
to trades more suited to the landlocked,
sales and insurance. And yes, he's sold you
on everything ephemeral you can think of,
the flesh and its satisfactions, words
you can't get comfortable with.

Love—he's sold you that and you like it fine,
it seems to fit without asking too much
of your shoulders, the small of your back —
your credulity. But you're left with this feeling
that somehow the sea belongs in this story,
you ought to go back and rethink this.

Instead you visit the hero's father and fall
over mountainous piles of gem-dust
that sticks to your eyelids, stays
in your lifeline. Now
you must touch someone fast or you might
have to live this thing out to the end, but

there's no one left to touch in this story.
Only the stone. What was its name?
No matter. Call it an opal
(call it that for its color, its heat
or if you think there's sorrow coming).
Or call it a sapphire (call it that

if you've already found the flaw).
Whatever it is it's a touchstone now;

you've insured it for full value
and locked it away in a safe where
you'll find it tonight when you come
with your mask and your narrow-beam light

for a second story you hope will teach
something of silence or dust
or the coastline of hope.
You'll draw close to hear it begin,
and it will, but this time
you'll call it: *The Same Old Story*.

# The Face of the Idiot Moon

I.
A leaf-shape
forms the right eye.
A dead leaf, arrested
at the instant it settles
into the socket
of its leaf-shaped shadow.

II.
In the left eye: something
unsettling, or yet to be settled.
Clearly an eye, no mistaking
that convex cut in the closed circle,
but it's flat-out empty,
no conventional fleck of light. Instead:
a white oval, wide with an idiot's
love for the flesh
of his own lower lip, for the wet
of his teeth, the bulge of his cheek—
his full face brimming
with idiot-love for the uncontained
idiocy of it all—the "it" that is only himself,
the "all" that is over.

III.
Any dolt could name this canvas: The Moon
As the World's Self-Portrait. A moron,
fat and blunt as a thumb. The face
of the imbecile child expectant mothers expect
in unsettling dreams that fall through cracks
in the blinds and lodge in the mind forever;
or the face of the killer the victim expects, armed
with a murderous lack of intention;

or the face of the lover we've all waited for,
the artist himself, who'll love us as we were meant
to be loved—out of shallow observance,
who'll love us because there is light and it falls
onto us, because there are eyes
and they open.

# If I get it wrong

it's because I know about the dead,
    that they are here, clayfoot,
        in an earth of names.

Scooping this future into my hands,
    I tighten around it, till clay sprouts
        from cracks in my fist,

spreads into wings, and breaks off. Shamed
    by the thin snake of silt in my palm,
        I wash it off.

Later, the women I come from call
    through the thick
        of things that are not

and do not have names.
    I watch their hands shape men.
        Wingless. Beautiful.

Beneath a triangle of stars
    I lay my hands open
        before them. Hands

are sacred, they tell me,
    even when they get it wrong.
        I get it wrong again and again,

as if men could be stone, could be angels.
    As if in our arms, or later, afloat
        in the floodwaters

of our dreams, men would not need
    to settle back, earthen,
        into the thick of things.

The women cleanse me, confirm me:
    dress me in earth-skins run through
        with the rhythms

of shadow; wash me in waters
    drawn from the roots
        of river-bed forests.

My hands grow certain. Until now,
    the paws of men have remained
        triangular, proof of their wanting

what is unheard of: an earth of their own
    names. They will have it soon.
        We will give them hands

when everything dangerous has been blunted,
    and love has taken the shape
        of what we have left

unsaid. *To make hands,*
    the women tell me now
        *is simple: take sweet tongue-silt*

*to the gathered muscles of shadows.*
    The men I make now are wingless.
        And their hands, their hands!

# Two-Part Meditation

I.

If you resist their avid, continuous hunger and don't
throw bread to the white-eyed churn, the flash of heads
like wedged wrenches, they'll simply
hang motionless there in the shade, inside
a nearly rippleless water below
the bridge in the Japanese Garden.
If you're alone
and look down and down for longer and longer,
the bridge will invert, the pool itself
will turn inside-out,
by a property of scale or light or the still
opacity of your eye:
the water, veinous and gilled; the fish,
borderless, rippleless currents of fishness,
washing up through a dark stillness
of visible time,
into your pure reception,
arriving in shades of tremble or shiver,
of heartmurmur, ripen or chime,
who can say? the words
are elsewhere,
and though the thought of scraping brings winces
(a mottled rawness, mauve, and your mind
snatched from there
to the why? of the document-world,
and the where-shall-I-go-now,-limping? eyes
of the torturer's daughter,
and the gritty imagined grate of blades
on grey pain-carrots), don't
give in to the mind's hunger
to hate, at times, itself. Hold out.
Try to touch, with the barest tip

of attention, this notion of scales
pried loose, unhinged from fishness,
releasing a floating refraction that falls up
into eyes held open, lidless,
eyes pried loose from a mind.
In the split-inch of time
before a heart darts in and is yours,
and your mind snaps back like a hinge,
like an avid fish to its food, while it's all
still beneath—and wordless: *This*
is the music he makes
in the small house not far
from my door.


II.

I've been reading of violets,
        a signature scent in invisible ink,
                containing its own disappearance.

Receptors receive it; it lingers;
        and then, by a property of the scent itself,
                erases all trace from our senses.

In this way, his music has moved all morning
        into and out of my consciousness,
                its muscle flow as controlled as a cat

on a stalk, growing closer, slow as bamboo,
        stretching a barely perceptible
                claw.

The quiet composer who disappeared
        into the small house not far from my door
                to amass and disperse, and at last erase,

these tonal clouds, is Japanese,
        which may explain
                my thoughts of the Garden.

How strange to follow the paths
        of our thinking. We, too, are creatures
                of figure and ground —

like a cat on the prowl, cautious, its paws
        always deep in the shadows
                of birds. And perhaps

this sensory self-effacement
        is pain's way too: only so much
                we can take before our receptors are full; we

pass out. Modulated, then, and erased
        by conductors beyond our control, we're allowed
                to form briefly, and only from time

to time, a sense of our lives,
        of where it hurts, and how much
                and what are the borders.

And when we've figured
        as best we can,
                by a property of the self itself,

we're erased, decomposed—ground again.

# Pentecost

I.
On this October Sunday I have come
home, in hot wind and blown-flame leaves,
to my old church:
old troubled wood of kneeler, altar,
cross; old rhythms of the heart, cast off
and echoing.

I kneel
for no reason I can name,
and nothing comes but the clear-eyed stare,
mastered through years of nothing to forgive
or be forgiven. On standards
against the far wall,

the women have hung the altar flags,
the seasons of the Christian year.
I find Epiphany's purple
and the bright darkness of Lent,
but another draws my eyes:
wild tongues, aflame on white felt.

Pentecost: I had forgotten.

II.
Downstairs, the Poetry Center holds
its meeting. A visiting critic advises us
to learn to write the sentence.
Clear. Precise. "The rest,"
he says, "we will be forgiven."
Not much of a promise.

Above, a service is beginning.
Funeral? Baptism?
Organ tones fall among us,
drowning whole lines, as one by one

we rise to read our poems,
taking on the outsized task

of talking ourselves down
from danger.
My mind wanders.
When I come to myself, my eyes
are fixed on the glass,
where leaves press, red

and fallen into beauty.

III.
"Chekhov,"
the critic reminds us, "claims
the hardest decisions come
at beginnings and ends, the places
we are tempted most
to lie."

My own openings
come easily these days,
but endings
are more troublesome,
arriving out of nowhere
like a black-sheep brother

wearing my face.
Or worse, they pin me blinking
in the crossbeams
of integrity and pain—
paralyzed again.
For such half-truths,

we cannot ask forgiveness.

IV.
Another poet falls silent.
We choose our words with care, wanting
to love each other's work, avoid judging.

Suddenly I think of sin—a thing
I've never believed in.
But tonight, I know I'll lie

alone in the dark, listing damages
my love has done.
Love, too, ends hard, a sentence
ill-begun and echoing on
in the hollow a silence makes
over long distance. Love, too,

not much of a promise.
In this year's Christian calendar,
the season for payment has passed,
but in the world
beyond this tall window glass,
leaves fall on every side—

alive and burning.


V.
Late tonight when leaves
have quieted themselves against my walls,
I'll listen to their whispered hush,
and hold myself accountable
for my own fall into a life
whose opening line I cannot check

for truth,
whose final line is the same lie
as every sentence
not yet over: *I may be wrong, but. . .*
an accurate sentence
that ends nothing.

The organ has fallen silent,
but we continue a cappella,
reading our lines as haltingly as ever,
trying with all our hearts to master
the difficult art of offering truth

and comfort,

in the same sentence.

VI.
It's our task, fallen to us
from the foreign tongue of a God
who goes on and on,
exacting our love in advance,
for His single promise:
to bring one sentence to an end

without lying.
Not much of a promise. But given us
in a voice that echoes above us even now
and may echo forever,
while below, as if to help Him keep
His word, we work,

unrepentant, on the wording
of the only sentence we'll believe
when it comes down on our heads
in flame:
that all is forgiven anyway,
and this long fall

is over.

# Draft of an Answer

Your letters, forwarded here from the South,
have found me at last, as Spring has found me,
a stranger, startled by my own possessions, aghast
at what I have over the winter lost track of
(the weight of blood in the chest, the fragile give
of the rib cage); aghast at earth's wide places
that seem designed, not for human shapes,
but for something vast that will move, horizontal,
upon her—like shadows or wind,
a glacial advance, or the slow spread
of seeds and attendant birds into the North.

I mention none of this in my letter; instead
I comment on the day's completions: the work
of the teapot and typewriter,
the trustworthy nature of the water heater,
the good behavior of motors—all things
proceeding as planned in this venture. And love
and regret, only an odd, lovely warp in the fabric
of my disappearance. I write that I'm looking forward
to home, your familiar face, sweet arms—but that
is looking back. Forward is farther North, my love,
into Winter's retreating shape, into ice.
Your letters, like Spring, have been forwarded here
by an error to find me a stranger, and, briefly,
in drafting my answer, I can't find a closing (yours?
yours truly?) or recall, for a moment, our home address.

# Intercession

A heavy dawn. A bird's
tireless monochrome —
four soundings, a pause, and four,
and on—till, startled, you notice
it's silent now—and has been.

Two fans of fungus, vertically aligned,
one on the living cedar, the other
below, on the dead, and how many times
did your eyes pass over, taking in both
as if you were viewing the same creature?

Or consider the way you've spoken
the same words over and over for griefs
no words should touch, or accepted
with equal gratitude, such vast
inequalities of pleasure.

And it matters little—the fact
that you never meant it. The patient,
plentiful world intercedes
with second chances, answering
blindness with stones

where blue moths pause,
fluted riffles in ditch water after
a morning of murmuring rain,
a flicker's looping flight, a lone
fat bee at the fence. And yes,

it may be forgiveness
you need, but not for this long
inattentiveness
as much as for these: your few
brief moments of knowing

(soon folded back

beneath the manifold tellings
of Time)
that you never meant
most of your life.

# After the Service

Light says its one thing: *many*. We rise
and go our ways. We can't help it.

But there is nowhere. Stasis, unbearable.
No one dying now, being born, in all the world. Stars

swallow back the light that belongs already to time.
Nothing breathes, the sea deepens itself imperceptibly, earth

settles, becomes one level way
that does not lead.

\*

How will this ever be completed? This dark.
Not mere *darkening*, which would be bearable. No, this is

the dark, too long a thing to think, too long
to give oneself to—like grief, or the idea of a life led.

One's self, too, so long a thing
it cannot be thought, has never been thought.

This is the dark's sway, the terrible equipoise
that cannot last. It cannot last, light says. We are

too many for it. We rise.
We go our ways.

# The One Art That Changes Nothing

The wire artist walks over broken glass
without falling, bleeds gold.

Beauty begins, she believes, in small stones—
deep red, bright blue—and grows into wings,

rising gold in the second fire, all things
from the three beginnings.

But soon she needs more, the splash and flourish
of Byzantine doings: azure and crimson,

against a stone-gold sky.
When all domes are rife with tiles, and nothing

looks real or within reach, she finds
more modest ways to fill space.

Back home in her own four chambers, she breathes
deeper, slower. After a time, her walls thin

to transparency, beat like wings,
and she thinks: pastels.

Limn the marble skies with streaks, she thinks,
or sprinkle sidewalks with random glints,

or fill—she has it now—windows with light;
paint glass with sprays of ice; leave sea-shapes

on shells, sky-shapes on feathers; let
the very air intimate, until all meaning disappears

abruptly into noon. All this she does, but soon
the light thins. Then she learns tropism, leans

like the leaf's green heart toward the west, where,
on the wire horizon, light walks broken glass,

bleeding on the stones. She, too,
works endangered, now, passing into midnight

where her self escapes her. She sees
no form, knows no line—and walks it,

faithfully serving the one art she knows
changes nothing—into nothing else.

# Facing Pages

Five AM,
sky black at the glass;
outside, the rise of wind, or the rush
of leaves against my walls.
I curl in the rocker, whispering Rilke,
*Herbsttag* and *Abend*,
in facing translations.

From opposite pages,
the paired lines slant their two
intentions toward a shadowed center.
Above them my voice floats its hope
of equivalent meanings; doubt
curves a wide path of sadness
through what I think I know.

And all the while the world is leaving
the dark, making its way back,
underwater like a willful child
holding his breath,
while grown-ups on the bank lean in
toward a shadow
dragged over the black lakebed.

Too long. And then,
a pulse; the surface breaks.
I feel it now, that lift of skin.
The thing, beginning. At the glass,
dark limbs cut themselves back into the world:
thin tributaries down which local names
flow again: *Sweet gum. Oak.*

Words stir in me with no large intention,
only to enter, to say what it's like here: a few
last leaves impaled on spokes of gold, the glass
of the neighbor's high windows,

baring the sun.
*Dawn.* Call it *dawn.* Again.
The thing and the waiting aligned. Named.

*Dawn.* I take up my accustomed task,
cut lengths of breath and space,
match consonants, search for a rich
fortuitous twinning of vowels, translating
the light of my two lost countries.
The wedge of each match reopens
the world's oldest wound.

*Dawn* after *dawn.*
The wonder is I keep at it,
though the heart sinks with each utterance,
as the world breaks always into the same
pieces, despite my large intentions,
my sense of exile, my dreaming
the endless poem Home.

*Dawn.* Above the facing pages
of what I think I know, the same words rise,
while beneath,
in the moist bed of the stilled tongue,
fertile and first,
the autistic sun breathes
underwater: the language,

the dark Undivided.

# About the Author

Marjorie Stelmach lives in St. Louis, Missouri, where she teaches at Ladue High School and Washington University. She has earned an MFA from the Washington University Writer's Program and has been a fellow at the Virginia Center for the Creative Arts. Her work has appeared in *Yankee, Southern Poetry Review, Union Street Review, River Styx, Webster Review, Ascent, West Branch,* and others. Her poems have received a number of awards including the *Malahat Review* Long Poetry Contest in 1990 and 1992, the first annual Missouri Biennial Award in 1988, the first *Chelsea* Award in 1988, and the Billee Murray Denny Award in 1987 and 1992.